I'm not your

paper princess

poems

j.r. rogue

I'm Not Your Paper Princess: Poems

Copyright © 2019 by J.R. ROGUE
Editor: Christina Hart

ISBN: 9781692137939

Princess Crown

she was born on a cloudy,
cold day in eighty-seven.
they cut her mother
open & pulled her out.
she didn't cry, & they didn't slap her.
they say she smiled.
she laughs at the story.

loved ones like you to believe you
were always strong.

that you weren't allowed to break.
I'm sorry my story wounded you.

she died on a sunny,
loud day in ninety-nine.
if they had cut her open
they would have found
a lukewarm heart & lungs
like deflated balloons.
why didn't I cry when he thieved?

her princess crown had fallen.
her limbs
were no longer marvelous things
that would carry her to far off places.
dirty things were not always dirty things.

My Depression Is So Damn Reliable

it feels like all the plates stacked
neatly in the cabinets are tumbling out,
& all the glasses are following suit.
everything is shattering inside my head
but I'm not downstairs,
I'm not in the kitchen.
I'm in my bedroom &
the shades are drawn.
it is a black cave
& I don't want anyone lying next to me.
my throat is closing but there are no tears.
I haven't showered in
two days; the dishes mock me.
my mouth is full of dirt
& the floor feels like ants
beneath my feet.

I'm trying to figure out how you can
feel so alone
with so many voices swirling around you,
when you're never alone;
when everything you've ever hated about
yourself enters the room like a stranger,
sits down like a lover,
breaks bread like a family
member about to
tell you the cancer has won.

Miami

tell me what it tastes like—
your soul in reverse.
spit it out & spout off every
sticky little word they like.

go easy, that ass is bruised
& your lips are chapped.
save some face paint
for the rest of the line.

a pinch of sex, a dash of harassment,
they fit fine in your coat sleeve.
no one will see.

your mouth, the dexterity,
I'm astounded!
"he's just a flirt &
this meal didn't cost me a dime."
eat up, don't save any for me.

your yesterday screams still
ricochet back   forth
& 'round & 'round
in my cranium.

but I'm reading about the
laughing man's death

& pushing them all out.

because, *shhhhh,* you told me to never tell.
&, *shhhhhh,* you told me you were *fine.*
yes, *shhhhhh,* you'll *have my back next time.*

"give me your daily special."

tell me what selling out tastes like.

Pause & Repent

someone said the penitent woman
shall be worshipped.
  you asked for it.
  you wanted it.
  why did you dress
  that way?
  why did you drown
  clear eyes?

someone said the penitent woman
shall appease the masses.
  you are a toy.
  you are a tease.
  you belong
  to these dogs,
  these animals,
  these thieves.

  repent.
  repent.
  repent.

have you researched the
repercussions of excessive drinking?
have you practiced your clear "no" & a
proper lady's behavior today?

repent.
repent.
repent.

have you ever wanted
to set the world on fire?

so have I.

Petals

paper thin pre-adolescent
skin meant for playgrounds
& paddling pools
where predators
prey & press
their poison into
their petals
while praying to
remain
unimprisoned.

Stone in my Gut

as a little girl,
I was infatuated with princesses.
finding true love was a strength
I desired above all else.
        gold glitter,
        pressed lips,
        & *forever* princes,
                I needed it.

happily-ever-after is sold pretty early,
pretty easily to pretty little girls with
big brown eyes & mute mouths.

I found my old journals the other day.
half a lifetime ago
I held hope in my palms,
        let it spill—
        pages,
        cupped hands,
        strong boys' lips as they gripped
        my virgin hips.

I can almost taste my hope
& innocence in those poems.
I can almost believe
that I was once a different girl.

when I was that young girl,
writing close to her bedside lamp,
my mother was sleeping alone.

she was waking at dawn,
shoveling dog shit.
she was walking me & my brother
down our long country road to the bus.

she was brushing my hair before bed.
she was wiping my tears
        when the kids at school
        called me
        skank, trailer trash, dirty.

she was pissing me off,
telling me I couldn't leave the table
until I ate my peas.

she was the same age I am now;
        holding two kids together,
        falling apart in her bedroom, alone.

she was stitching a safe
world into my spine.

she was the same age I am now &
I can't figure out how she did it.
I can't figure out how she gets softer,
while I feel more stone in my

gut each waking day.

there is a strength in that.
I desire it above all else.

Faceless Woman

so how did I end up here?
lost & losing who I am.
the mirror is a thief;
I am an accomplice to
these crimes.

my days start off as days
& remain as footnotes,
deleted scenes,
forgotten flashbacks.

how did I end up there?

I kiss you & there is no static,

there is no swelling music.
I thought this was romance,
but I am so wrong,
so very hopeful & trying.

will you love the side character?
the extra, the cut-out faceless woman?

how did we end up here?

What The Fuck are You Crying For?

so it's a Tuesday.
it's always a Tuesday.
some old man tells you how pretty you are.
you don't smile.
you take three showers.
you cry & you don't tell anyone
because *what the fuck are you crying for?*
your uncle hugs you on Sunday at dinner
without warning.
he approaches from behind.
you're on top of it all that day.
your performance: perfection.
no one knows you threw up in the bath-
room.
you kiss your mother after you suck
on an after-dinner mint until it is all milk
& mask in your mouth.

you leave;
you are slow motion,
salt, static—
standing still.

no one sees.

Breakings

I have thrown out two dictionaries
looking for it;
a word for the way
we hold on to each other
knowing how needful our ending is,
throbbing in the distance.

it's funny how my life
looks in this mirror.

this funhouse tragedy.
everything is amplified.

my face isn't laughing
but someone is in the background.

breakings are echoes.

I was not meant for this,
but I keep finding myself here.

I imagine you are what addiction tastes like.
kissing you is a slow drag,
so is leaving,

though I never know how to make it stick.

breaking you is an addiction.
we both know my blood is boiling for this,
is never going to find mending for this.

you say you're stuck between
a rock & a hard place.

I wish I knew which one I was.
I wish I was neither,
but the soft place to land when
this is all too much.

I wish I knew how to write poetry
about something other than
my maniac heart,
my blank stare,
my loud void.

The Debt for Happiness

is it any wonder
the debt was too much?
your white sea eyes draw
wide at my audacity.

I am not a smile
but a terror
in all my wrongness.

it is a marriage made
in Pluto's honor,
for happiness that you
cannot comprehend,
the breed tailored true to me.

you are lousy with false
acceptance, petals
I will not pick from
your outstretched hands.

is it any wonder
we outgrew each other?

Garden Girl

I have been punishing myself again.
two weeks in a row.
you say it's fine,
you don't need me to be a garden,
but the whole world wants
me to be a garden.
they want me to have ivy hair
& rose-bud lips.
they want root legs & for the
wandering to wither.

I am withered.
I am where dead things come to rest.

there is nothing left
of nurturing in my belly.

this is fine, but you do not think it is fine.
I have been punishing myself again,
thinking of your subtle punishing.

I think of ten years from now.
I think of resentment & how
we will let it slide into our bed.

I think of letting you go,
so you can find a garden girl.

some garden girl to give
you everything you deserve.

Violent She

violet she, all the colors
I cannot create crawl from her pores,
skin to skin you drink them in.

songs say rainbows
rip from her seams,
cover the city streets in lazy laughs.

the ruse reeks, I taste the
chorus & weaken.

this is the ugly in me.

I'll sacrifice her stealing soul.
she has what I can never again touch.
I'll build the pyre higher.
~~violent me~~ violent she, all the night
you choke to swallow.

I'll wrap her in my reverse wishes,
wanting witchcraft,
rip you from her cunt,
pull your puppet strings.

we'll dance the way
we do in my dreams.
you'll love me again, you'll see.

Temptation Between My Teeth

he claimed he could find
something more
vulgar than
my tongue getting over you

until
he tasted it.

Two Lies on a Sunday

I can move past this.
it's only a heart wound.

I like to lie to myself,
it's a fun trick,

a shy pastime of mine.

you loved it, too.
the way a lie would taste
on my lips when I would kiss you.

I don't love you.
I said it like a joke,
because we both knew
it would never be true.

I didn't know lovers could
use those secrets against
you until I met you.

until you met her.

Cupping Ignorance

I have grown tired
of trying to explain this to you.

my lover told me people can interpret
art any way they please,
& it doesn't matter what I meant it to be.

that makes me sad,
but I know he is right.

I cannot cup ignorance to my hands
& breathe it brilliance.

I can paint this any way I like.

& no matter what,
my vulnerability will make
you shudder.

it will make you clutch
your coat, hope your own
demons aren't pushing their way out,

trying to shake hands with mine.

Paper

they tell me to write the villain in.
make her made of the vile.
give her a snake tongue,
a red whisper,
sex dripping.

there is a hush to her laugh,
the curve of her foot fits into his palm,
he is unmoved by her seamless flaws.

she cries when it rains.
she has his mother's patience.
she will steal him & I will not blame him.

they tell me to write a villain
& I still taste the glue,

move with the paper dress.

So You Know What I Feel Like

you like to tell me I'm soft.
but you're not talking about the sex.
I was there, & I know I wasn't soft.

you have these eyes,
they reach through state lines.
mostly you piss me off,
because hiding from you never works.
on odd days, you send me songs.
you told me about a mountain near your
childhood home that I should climb.

you said you would never lead me on,
but friendship with you is such a turn-on.

I know I'm doing this wrong,
but at least I'm honest.
yes, I try to hide from you,
but at least I'm always true.
I know I'll survive this if you
never want me the
way I've always wanted you.

Purple Is The Sky

purple is the sky
on her thigh
that you have canvased
like an astronomer.

you pull your brush,
your mouth,
from her form & smile
with picket fence teeth
you never meant to scare
her with.

she smiles back, like
a woman in & out
of love-adjacent
feelings for you & maybe
some other men.

purple is the sky of her eyes
when she looks at you
& you forget
all the rest.

I Wish They Would Stop Romancing Me

no, he wasn't the first to try to fuck
his way into my poetry,
& I doubt he will
be the last.

Laugh

being what you
need me to be
has become exhausting.
exhausting, what
a word
so lacking,
so barren, like me.

you say you feel lonely
when you are with me.

I am lonely when I am with me.
why won't you let me leave?
do you love the pain?

maybe that is the only thing
we have in common.
I can't even make you laugh,
what a sad thing to realize.

& you can't make me laugh,
another thing we have in common.

our bellies lacking,
so barren,
like our love.

Gatekeeper

my mother told me that
when I was a little girl
I came home crying from school one day.
I bawled & bawled until they sent me
home.

no one could ever figure out why.
                    & it was forgotten.

I wonder if it was the day after
    the pretty pink color of innocence
          was drained away.

I wonder who decides what
we forget,
& what
we hold onto.

"Was it Rape?"

there's something in the short swift
saying from your condescension,
your stained lips.
my underbelly is too neat.
it's a reversal.
a subtle summersault into accusations
I can't acquire a taste for.
I can't catch the dismount.
I can't quite fit into your palm.
what about my near-death offends you?
you're pondering approximate penetration,
playing it all out.
you knew a girl once who took it
a little harder than I did.
she was a little younger,
she got hurt a little more,
cut a little deeper.
you miss her & you're eyeing the
chalk outline over my shoulder,
wrapped around my shadow.
you pick the corn kernel from your teeth.
brass knuckles & bent knees for the climax.

"no," I say.

so you say I'll be okay.

When October Comes

I will breathe amber wings.
I will unfurl.
I will open my mouth
& her name will fall out, into my lap.
I will comb her hair.
I will press her tiny boots to my temple,
listen to where she has walked.
when October comes,
I will fold her clothes
in the rain.
I will open my mouth
& she will call me Mother,
shush me.
I will be all that you wished I could be.

Home Run

I like to tell the boys who are
villains that they remind me of home.
I like to tell them this & hide my smile.
they think home is a special thing,
some wondrous thing,
some way I'm saying they're staying.
but to me home is slammed doors
& no words between mothers & fathers.
home is fending for myself.
wine coolers on the lawn.
curfews I never broke because
I stole out the window.
home is hoping your bedroom
door knob doesn't turn.
home is a prison & I'm not quite free of it.

Feather

there's an anvil
sitting on my chest
disguised as a feather,

but I know better.

As Everything Turns Grey

you rip your chest open,
exposing all
the vulnerable
parts inside to the
shadows
painting our room in
bottomless depths of honesty.
their relentless workings echo
back & forth,
boomerang against our
bedroom walls.
I dip my fingertips
in & brush them over the
red wires,
the humming hues
too vibrant for the
noir choking
the light away.
as everything
turns to grey
you break open
& show
me light
in ways the
waking sun never can.

The World

the world weighs on me,

heavy socked feet dancing
absurdly on piano strings.

Loud Days

I pressed the blade just a little
bit deeper underneath my fingernail.
I just needed a little bit of red
to complete the picture in
my mind.
I just needed a
little bit of blue to ease off
of my eyes.
I just needed
your memory to quit
fucking me for one
goddamn moment.

we're always making
art, even on my
loudest days.

Princess To Queen

I told him nothing
made me happy anymore.

I thought he could
see right through me,
that he could feel my emptiness.

but he couldn't.
I am the illusionist.
I am the queen of this game.

We Are So Far From Our Dreams

from the way we planned.
vacations we could not afford.
homes we could never
stomach the mortgage for.
window shopping for a life that
would never be ours,
but we dreamed it
that way at night,
clutched close to each other.
like we could start a fire
between us,
bring life forth from it,
not destruction.
this can't be us,
the past tense, can it?

I have no free will, I am a
victim of this sorrow.
some bed-ridden former self.
some version of me that you
would never love,
but you decided not to love
the real me anyway.

we are so far from all we wanted;
all I thought you wanted, too.

Inverted Images

he has a wide mouth, lips.
so many lips, it seems
there is a baritone saxophone
in his stomach.

when he tells me stories, I actually listen.
it's manners, I remind myself.
you always scolded me when
I ordered a double stack from Wendy's
& didn't say thank you to the
drive-thru attendant.

his skin is tan, even in the winter,
eyes blue, no black holes to slip
into on a Sunday night.

he has a wide mouth,
& I want to fall into it.
so many hips & sheets.
denial tastes like him,
his coffee-stained
end table in his room,
with the light bulb blown out.

I can't leave until he falls asleep.
it's manners, you taught me that.

you didn't leave until I was warm
& safe, soft asleep,
thinking you would come back home.

In The Pursuit Of Nothing

so you kiss him.
& you take him home.
or you let him take you home.
it doesn't matter really, it's all the same
& the numbing comes from all sides.

he tastes like peppermint,
like honey whiskey.
like the vodka on your tongue.

he tastes like an escape.
he tastes like rebounding the right way,
because that's not what this is.

you cannot drown out the drums,
the heartbeats.
the remembrance of what
he took from you.

the records on the front lawn,
the shirt he left behind.
the toothbrush you lost, replaceable,
but always on your mind.

the blue color. the fresh bristles.

you kiss him

& it's a blackout, a hum.
it's a bandaid,
& you just don't care.

.

The Taste Of Time

you built
a matchstick house
at the back
of my throat.

I liked the taste
of your anger.

smoke out the
remains of last night.

smoke out the times
I said I would leave.

smoke out who we
used to be.

Void

this is what I'll always have on her.
the mystery.
the mystery of you & me.
she had you.
you never had me.
this is all I'll ever have on her.
she had the home.
your heart & family.

I have the mystery.
I have this hope that you
wonder about me.

that her void leaves
you lonely, leaves room for me.

Chalk Line

you are the window;
I see the world through your young eyes,
& maybe that is what always
pulled me to you.

soft laugh & hard past;
hard heart & soft belly.

you are not the knife,
though I cut myself on you.

I can feel you lingering
in the deep pools of my regret.

I wish we never met;
I wish the touch of hands
could rewind to the place
where our words first collided.

we could be so much more
than the expanse,
the over exposure
we faded out into.

you are the balcony;
I am the chalk line below.

I can feel you lingering
in my belly,

deep in the
places we never
should have met.

J.R. Rogue first put pen to paper at the age of fifteen after developing an unrequited high school crush & has never stopped writing about heartache.
She has published multiple novels & volumes of poetry.

J.R. ROGUE is very active on social media & encourages you to follow her around.
www.jrrogue.com
contact@jrrogue.com

also by j.r. rogue

Novels
Burning Muses
Background Music
Kiss Me Like You Mean It
I Like You, I Love Her
The Rebound

Novellas
Teach Me

Poetry
La Douleur Exquise
Tell Me Where It Hurts
An Open Suitcase & New Blue Tears
Rouge
Apus
Le Chant Des Sirènes
Letters to the Moon
All Of My Bullshit Truths: Collected Poems
Exits, Desires, & Slow Fires
Breakup Poems
I Have Sold A Beautiful Lie

Secrets We Told The City
w/Kat Savage